# VENICE
## *from the air*

This book is dedicated to Gisella

─────────────

**Pages 4–5:** *If you wanted to experience the sensation of seeing Venice from a ship's prow, the far corner of the Dogana da Mar would do the job. On the tower two telamons hold up a golden ball upon which Fortune poses, turning with the wind.*

**Venice from the Air**
Translated from Italian by David Bloom

© Times Editions 1988
422 Thomson Road, Singapore 1129

First published in the United States of America in 1988 by
Rizzoli International Publications, Inc.
597 Fifth Avenue, New York, NY 10017

Printed by Tien Wah Press, Singapore
Colour separation by Far East Offset, Malaysia
Typeset by Superskill Graphics, Singapore

ISBN: 0-8478-1018-6
LC: 88-43022

# VENICE
## *from the air*

Photographed by Guido Alberto Rossi
Text by Franco Masiero

*Rizzoli*
NEW YORK

# Contents

Who is she—this Venice?
Queen of the waves but
under the peremptory
command of the ebb and
flow of tide and light?
**Pages 6-7:** *Children of the
sea, Venetians have ruled
the waters in and outside
of Venice's embrace.*
**Pages 8-9:** *A cabin on stilts
along a canal, grass strug-
gling out of muddy islets,
the geometric rhythms of a
fish-breeding plant, a purely
linear horizon—the Laguna
as it has always been.*
**Pages 10-11:** *The Arsenal
rose in front of the island of
San Pietro di Castello in
1104. For centuries this
was the biggest factory
in the world.*

What are the deep reasons, the essential laws, which govern this apparent confusion of straight and crooked, high and low, void and full? The reasons are of the water, its ebb and flow and play with the light.

15

# BRIDE OF THE SEA

This book is built on air; it flies, with curiosity and even indiscretion, over the naked form, disguised from the ground, of Venice; it hems her about, it takes her measure, it asks her to display herself just as she is, to tuck no secrets away from us. In a way it is also a book composed of caresses, hovering as it does over the city's overripe but still-lovely body. Out of air it constructs an immaterial context of time and space in a provisory place of trompe l'oeil games played on land and water with a constantly changing light: the result is that elusive illusion which we like to call beauty.

It began with a mighty arc of mountains, the Alps. Spring each year took its snows and turned them to rivers, pouring them down to the sea. The rivers picked up stones, mud, rubble along the way and deposited them in the gulf where, over millennia, the Padan Valley formed. The great river, slowly now, wound its way to the sea, leaving behind the finer sands. The tides shoved the sand back, crushing the fan of the rivermouth and creating fine tongues of beach around a host of islands in a network of canals in the vast internal basin we call the Laguna.

This was and remains an unstable place, subject to constant mutation; land and water wage a continual struggle for a tenuous dominance. Here is set the story of a people destined for a place like this: the hard story of an ungenerous country, a place that is almost not there at all, hidden under a veil of water or mixed into a swampy sort of impasto. Yet these people must have seen some kind of generosity there, because they entrusted themselves to it, relying on their own strength and keeping their stern eyes fixed on a future of greatness.

Time-travelling through the historical record, our first glimpse of Venice sounds like one of the tales of Odysseus: "While opposing winds shook the sea, Cleonimus the Spartan gained the coast of the Veneti with his Greek ships. He ordered some men to explore the area; they reported that the first thing they saw was a soft beach, just a strip of sand covered with dunes, brush and pine trees. Somewhat further they found swamps communicating with the sea and, beyond that, cultivated land as far as the distant and obscure forms of hills. It was a broad rivermouth. The Spartan saw that he would be able to bring the fleet to safety from the sea here and ordered the ships to enter the river." This is the narrative of an episode from 302 BC, written by the Roman historian Titus Livius, and

it is our earliest evidence of the Laguna's appearance in ancient times. And this brief description is all we know of how the lagoon looked, only twenty centuries ago.

Cleonimus, luckily, was a pleasing character. All he needed was shelter for his ships after a long stormy voyage; and indeed he arrived in Venetia stripped of rhetoric, in what was to become the true Venetian style, as opposed to the honeyed ecstasies of so many enchanted tourists. Such was the style of a hard, tenacious people who could transform what looked like a fairly bleak and hungry destiny into the history of grandeur of the thousand and more years of La Serenissima Repubblica di Venezia, rich, free and powerful, though her star too would ultimately sink, like those of every other empire.

Venice has always experienced storms, those that arose spontaneously from nature and those of the forces of history. The city was born just because the lagoon was there, and it could never have existed without it. The only way to understand anything about all this is to turn with deep attention, and as much humility, to those islets and canals, which seem so geographically abandoned while in fact making up the weft and warp of this eternal mirage.

A historical account, founded on such materials as are available, might begin around the eighth century BC, when populations from Illyria, Greece and Asia Minor, pushed by migrations from the north into their own territories, discovered a favourable climate, fresh water and arable land around the lagoon. After inevitable collisions with a sparse indigenous population the new arrivals settled in, and the tribes blended. As Rome to the south was undergoing its early expansion, the Venetian mainland witnessed the birth of a Veneto—Euganeo—Middle Eastern group with usages, rituals and customs of its own, living, probably, on fishing and agriculture.

Next came Roman civilization itself when, to counter the invasions of northern barbarians, Latins built the Aquileia Fortress and other installations along the edges of the lagoon. Of these the pre-eminent one is the harbour of Altino, vital in providing a link between Italy and the Danubian basin. With the Augustan Empire, Veneto and Istria became the Tenth Region of Rome; the territory around the Laguna became the focus of more and more important roads, and numerous urban centres blossomed in the area. In the surrounding countryside, and perhaps on some of the tiny lagoonal islands, arose the exquisite patrician villas that so astounded the poet Martial. Dams,

*Can Venice really be so beautiful? It is, in the magnificent architecture of the Basilica della Salute ("Basilica of Health"). In the aftermath of a dreadful plague, the erection of a church to the Virgin was decreed in 1603; the commission went to Baldassare Longhena and it took a good 56 years to complete the work.*

17

reclamations and canal works extracted ever more cultivable land from the lagoon.

Trying to picture the Venezia of those times we might imagine a lagoon landscape sprinkled with peasant hovels and, where the soil of the islets was relatively less stingy, the occasional village set in an intricate network of rivers, canals, broad swamps and marshes. The inhabitants built houses right over the water, of wood, reed and mud, mostly on stilts to protect them from the changeful play of the tides. Some were fishers, hunters, or farmers, while others produced salt and managed the earliest mills.

But history can take a sudden violent turn, and when the Imperial seat moved to Byzantium things here began to fall apart. Roman power was no longer capable of containing the push of invaders and so, now and again, came armies of Franks, Goths, Huns, Ostrogoths, Lombards and others thrusting along the coastal mainland and seizing it. On the spot where Cicero's "flower of Italy, precious stone of the Republic" once stood, there was terror and destruction wrought by the irrepressible will of the peoples of the north. The Venetians were now a fugitive people choosing to flee into the inhospitable lagoonal territory rather than to succumb to the invaders. The great mud-flats and cane-breaks and the few cottages swarmed with refugees. At first they built only more wretched hovels of reeds and clay, then, after Agilulf's destruction of Altino in 601, the inhabitants of that wealthy and important town settled permanently on a few islets, bringing along blocks of stone, columns, statues, even bricks rescued from their city. Those bricks are in the primitive nucleus of Torcello, where a splendid church made out of them still stands today. Torcello, Ammiana, Burano, Murano, Mazzorbo and Constanziaco were boroughs of the lagoon, taking their name from the original quarters (sextants, to be exact) of Altino.

The whole coast from Grado to Ravenna, which is one long chain of lagoons, was to undergo two centuries of exhaustion, terror and despair. But this brutalized and oppressed people would not bow; instead of submitting to their fate they set about creating a new one. There were immense difficulties in building a life inside the lagoon, between uncrossable canals and broken muddy bluffs, but this was precisely what saved them; enemy armies stopped, perplexed, when they got there. The place itself, with the shifting sea-bottom, the yielding ground, and the impossibility of getting any stable bearings, barred them better

than a fortified wall would have done. Meanwhile the trees that had once beautified the mainland fields turned into pile embankments and bridge supports, the scattered houses joined together into hardworking little communities, and next to the original boroughs of the Altino refugees stood the new settlements of Eraclea, Grado, Rialto, Malamocco, Pellestrina and Chioggia.

The reasons for the existence of this lagoon world are still a mystery. The refugees might have succumbed to some more resolute invasion, or exhausted themselves in the stubborn will to make a habitation out of a wretched bog. But they survived. Certainly it would be rash to suggest that it all happened because these people were bewitched by the stunning landscape; we, today, can imagine the future city immanent in the ground and forget what a nervous, demanding, unstable little corner of earth it is, but they, in the middle of that continual shifting and instability, could not.

The great strength of the people was in knowing how to rise to the surroundings humbly and creativity, and they showed the same adaptability in confronting history. Venice is perhaps the only one of the world's ancient cities that has never possessed a city wall: not only because the waters defended her, but also because of the political neutrality she always chose, permitting her to deal with all, and profit, of course, from every favourable occasion. Her people learned their adaptability through having to measure themselves against the difficulties of water and mud, and they learned their open-mindedness in the daily need to overcome the unexpected. Brought up in a situation made violent by nature and history, they went in active pursuit of fortune, ably; they caught it on the strength of pure ambition; they prevailed every time over the power and cunning of others.

It is recorded that the city of Venice was founded on 25 March 421 on the Rialtine group of islets, but before Rivoalto (the original name for the archipelago) was to play a historic role, centuries of tortuous, bloody events had to pass, marked by the strife and tyranny that must have animated the peoples pushed by barbarian fury into the lagoon. A unitary state grew very slowly from the congeries of settlements. At the time of election of the first Doge, Paoluccio Anafesto, in 697, the territory was still under Byzantine rule. But the Bosphorus was too far off to interfere with the enterprise of the Veneti. The first ducal seat was Eraclea, from which the honour passed to Malamocco, which has remained a most modest settlement since 810, when Pepin, son of Charlemagne, destroyed it in order to take possession of the Laguna. This was the circumstance that led to the choice of Venice as capital: the small Rialtine archipelago was the most isolated, and it was cut by an ample bend in a river that was very easy for the local boat traffic to navigate. This branch of the River Brenta was to become the Grand Canal.

By now the primitive economic activities had been supplemented by much more profitable ones; the extraction of salt was becoming a flourishing business and a fleet of ships catered to transport along the whole internal waterway-network between Aquileia and Ravenna. With the continual growth in maritime and commercial enterprise, the Venetian fleet constantly enlarged its own routes, toward Sicily and Africa, in the Tyrrhenian Sea, and much of the Levant.

It took four centuries to transform a tide of refugees into a people capable of defeating the King of the Franks and to make Venice a capital. Two more elapsed before the city grew to the point of imposing itself as the great Mediterranean power. After the year 1000, the modest bride of the sea became a queen. The Doge, with a great cortege of ships, aboard the state barge *Bucentaur*, decorated in Byzantine splendour, gave the water a golden ring: "We wed thee, sea, in token of true and perpetual dominion." It was the end of the saga of poverty and fear. No more barbarian armies came forward to try to conquer her, not even pirates dared to rob and rape within the lagoon. Meanwhile, the city subdued an enormous inland domain, and Istria and Dalmatia came under the Venetian yoke. The Crusades were a very good stroke of business for the city: the Fourth in particular put the seal on her grandeur, when, having furnished 300 ships to the expedition, Venice was able to subordinate its goals to her own wishes, and got an incommensurable profit out of the sacking of the Byzantine capital.

Even today it is possible to see, in so many parts of the city, the trophies of this unprecedented looting, in which it might be said that if Venice became figuratively a bit of the Orient, quite a bit of Constantinople literally became part of Venice. Bride of the sea, lady of the Levant, concubine of whomever was disposed to trade with her, the city became an emporium of precious goods that she then resold at a superb premium to all the peoples of Europe. Her fleets, two hundred ships strong at a time,

This Venetia of Franz Hogenberg dates to the year 1672, and it recalls many other models of the same period. In the centre of the legend, the elegantly framed paper gives a rendering of the progress of the Doge with the other dignitaries, and it is furnished with the insignia of command of the Republic.

travelled all the routes of the Mediterranean and the Atlantic coast under the guidance of expert sailors and unmatched merchants, while pepper, spices and every kind of costly product (down to a never entirely abandoned commerce in slaves) made *La Serenissima Repubblica di Venezia* a power to be envied and feared by the greatest.

It was not only precious merchandise that travelled on these ships, procured with skill and knowledge by merchants who were ready for anything "in the name of God and a good profit": every kind of person was on board—pilgrims, adventurers, ladies in search of Oriental novelties, ambassadors, mountebanks, spies, intriguers of every background, scholars sincerely looking for new discoveries and for contacts with the cultures of every different people particularly those of the East. It was with a proudly sophisticated self-awareness that the city maintained her reputation for uniqueness in beauty as in power, with an intelligent blending of European tradition and Asian ways into a complete palette of the possible shades of grace and harmony.

If she gave considerable attention to the constant building up of her own splendour, she reserved an equal amount to maintain the delicate balance of the lagoon— and thus to the fundamental requirement of *La Serenissima's* existence. As is always the case in nature, the same elements that created her are the ones that can destroy her. The Republic intervened endlessly with defensive works to consolidate the beaches and dykes to hold the river waters on paths that took them harmlessly out to sea. Sometimes the engineers made the right choices, but it happened also that they committed errors that had a negative effect on the equilibrium: many flourishing islands ended up surrounded with stagnant water, the source of barrenness in the soil and malaria among the inhabitants. Some of these can be seen today as little outcroppings of earth without any life whatever, while others have disappeared altogether, like Ammiana and Costanziaco, their whereabouts no longer even known for certain. To get an idea of the process go to Torcello: formerly a self-contained city of perhaps more than 30,000 and an episcopal see for some 1,000 years, it now has two churches, a house here and there, a bit of cultivated land and fewer than a hundred inhabitants. Still immensely beautiful, no doubt, it is an island that has been dead for centuries.

The drastically definitive solution was realized between the fifteenth and seventeenth centuries: diverting all the rivers outside the lagoon basin. Once more on this occasion the Republic showed her fidelity to her own principles, which, if they assured each citizen of the maximum liberty and tolerance, also made unconditional demands of respect and obedience to the State. Indeed there was a law punishing anyone who, outside those employed on the diversion works, spoke or wrote about them, with a heavy fine. The contemporary face of the lagoon, then, is especially the result of these decisions; afterwards further interventions were necessary, however, and occasional modifications have continued up to the painful and dangerous crisis of the present.

In between, the golden centuries went by; the lazy bend in the Brenta adorned itself with incomparable beauty, and the main piazza took on its definitive shape with the construction of its major jewels, the church of San Marco and the Palace of the Doges. *La Serenissima* ruled over vast territories on the mainland and dictated the law of the Mediterranean. Exceedingly substantial family fortunes established themselves and grew, creating the dramas of life in the pompous palaces. It was at this time that the form of Venice became what it is today. Then, the rise and consolidation of the various European nations determined the beginnings of decadence. The discovery of the New World and the establishment of oceanic trade routes were brutal blows to the city's economy; the Mediterranean was no longer the centre of the world, and Venice was doomed to decline. Her immense riches, her diplomatic and military skills, permitted her to stretch the end out over a long period: a tremendous *festa* that lasted for centuries, the last noble act of her happy history. She yielded bit by bit, first graciously, then abandoning herself to an unbridled desire to enjoy every step to extinction. She squandered everything for a magnificent appearance, aged rapidly as she tried to look lovelier—and succeeded, bewitching inhabitants and visitors with infinite cunning. She can still succeed, in spite of mistakes, and her shameless surrender to the most unbecoming carelessness.

In May 1797, a vile man, the last of the Doges, Ludovico Manin, convocated the Great Council, the highest authority of the State, for the last time. The Council that made Venice great when her citizens were men without scruples or fears decreed the end of the Republic, and submitted to the will of Napoleon Bonaparte.

He, Napoleon, played a not insignificant part in the shaping of modern Venice. He commanded the demoli-

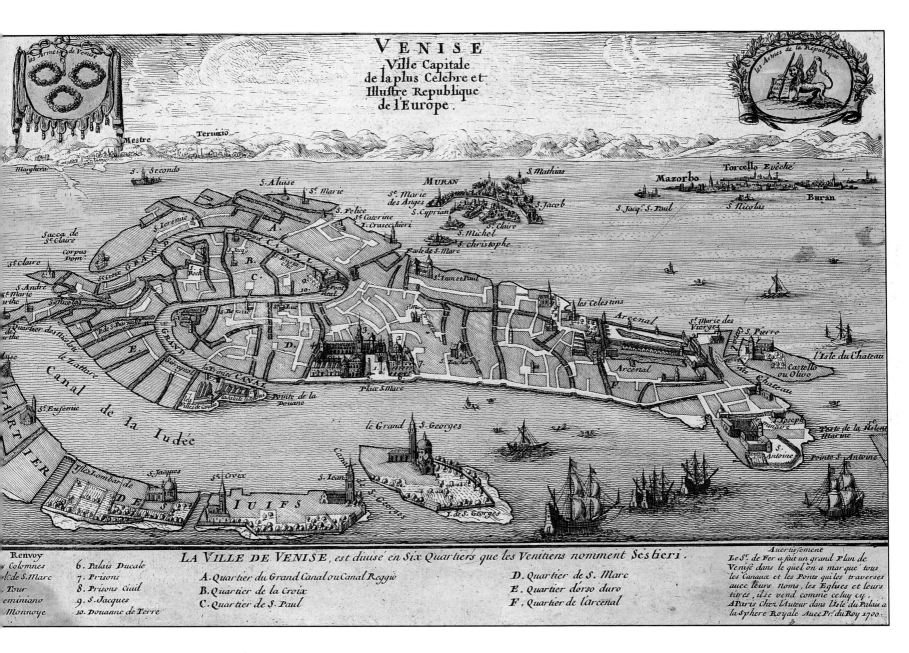

A synthetic image of the form of Venice in 1700, a little before the city was to take
on some of its modern character—just one bridge on the Grand Canal, no road link
with the mainland, and two separate islands (San Michele and San Cristoforo)
instead of the one destined to be the local cemetery.

23

tion of numerous buildings, especially ecclesiastical ones; he tried to steal a number of the principal works of art of the city; he introduced the period of Austrian dominance with his diplomatic policy, and this led to other modifications; not always negative ones, it must be said, in particular when we consider the great works of systematization in the lagoonal equilibrium.

But it was also the nineteenth century in which a living city, created in the first place by and for its citizens, became possessed by the idea of transforming itself, bit by bit, into its own mythical image, for display to the rest of the world. And it was the Romantic century that assembled the now-famous image of the decadent city, symbol of sorrow and death, voluptuously corrupt, the turbid tomb of blighted loves and helpless ghosts.

Shall we consider her in the transformations marked by aerial views drawn in the course of the centuries? We see first of all a lean Venetia, nearly nothing but the essence, with clear signs of rectilinear canals and large empty spaces; round about are the contrae, the outer districts: that is, all the principal islands like a diadem around her. Then comes the Venetie of the year 1500, a splendid image of the city at the point of greatest refulgence: dominating at the top is Neptune, king of the sea, and all around are the eight winds blowing as if to stir up the surface of the Laguna. The form of Venice appears fixed and stolid, and yet there is a perfect clarity in the details, and the Basin of San Marco is dense with ships: the city is truly alive.

In the title Plan of the Illustrious City of Venice the Dominant there is something pompous, laughable, a mockery: it is 1779, and the end is very near. No longer is the artist's admiring hand guided by the light of science, what we have here is rather a diligent but wholly ungifted printer. The same may be said for the Map of the City of Venice, a precise piece of observation devoid of all emotion. At last the naked truth: Topophotographic Relief of Venice, 1911, in which the city, delineated with an absolute clarity and an absolute anonymity, appears to lie under water, a purely geological object to which chance has given the form of the city that was, once, Venice.

Now let us consider her better, Venice, photographed from the air with love, and rich with all those colours that still clothe her with charm. We fly, with curiosity and even indiscretion, to gather her in our embrace—to display herself just as she is , to those of us that know what she was. Will it be our turn to love her once more, this Venice?

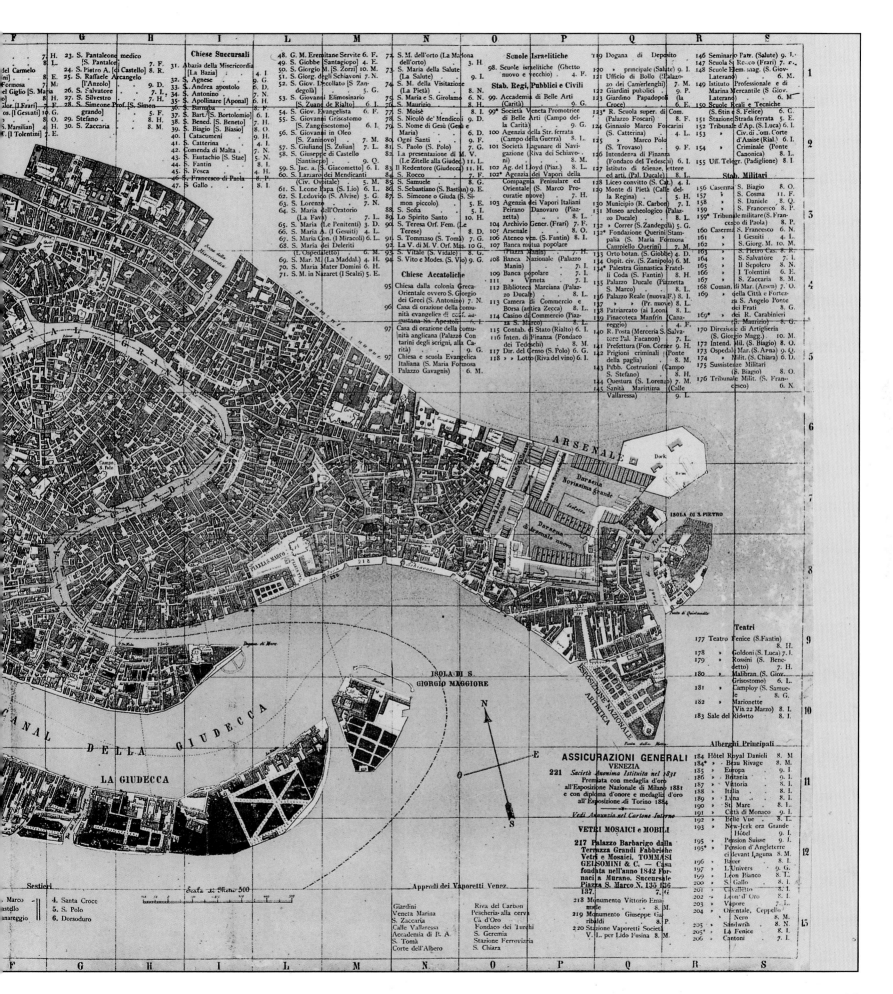

# THE CITY AND THE SHADOW

"Venice ... is still left for our beholding in the final period of her decline: a ghost upon the sands of the sea, so weak—so quiet,—so bereft of all but her loveliness, that we might well doubt, as we watched her faint reflection in the mirage of the lagoon, which was the City, and which the Shadow." (John Ruskin, *The Stones of Venice*, v. 1)

But what was Venice? After the hard times of the origin, of the flight into the Laguna, around AD 1000 the city had already become a duchy: we can imagine, within today's profile, a series of emergent and in some sense inhabited areas. The six boroughs, the *sestieri*, must have existed already, in embryonic form: Olivolo at the northeast end, where San Pietro di Castello and the Arsenal now stand; Gemini, northeast facing the Basin; Rivoalto, where San Marco is and along the Grand Canal to beyond the Rialto Bridge; Luprio, along the two banks of the Grand Canal at the point where the modern city is at its widest; Canaleclo, toward the northwest border; and Dorsoduro, on the southern flank by the bridge of the Accademia and the tip of the Dogana. In front, beyond the canal of the Giudecca (it was called Vigano then), Spinalonga, one tract of today's La Giudecca, and the island of San Giorgio rose from the water.

On this landscape of emerging ridges, with sections of mud and cultivated fields separated by more or less vast marshes, were scattered or grouped houses. The shores were held up and protected by wooden palisades or embankments or rushes against excessive erosion. Wood must have dominated a list of construction materials except for the occasional building intermingling stone and bricks picked up from the sites of ruins.

At the point where the canal meandered into its tightest curve, perhaps just at the point where it ceases to be effectively navigable, people were constructing the commercial neighbourhoods: Rialto, where the agricultural produce of the Realtine estuary converged, with butcher's meat and other goods. Nearby as the crow flies, less than 600 metres, truck gardens stretched over the area we see as Piazza San Marco. On the edge there were buildings by now destined to be important: the castle that was to become the splendid Palace of the Doges, and the church that already housed the remains of its protector, Saint Mark, stolen with rapacious political foresight from his tomb in distant Alexandria. A canal ran in front of the church's facade, and where the piazzetta is now with its two grand columns must have been a bit of lagoon. Here and there along the perimeter of the gardens of San Marco stood houses on a series of arches: these were eventually the supremely elegant prospect of the Procuratie.

By the twelfth century the city was already a power inland and on the trade routes to the Levant. Its general shape, henceforth, would not change much, though so far it was still slender. On the other hand its intense urbanization was shown by 88 churches, and, measuring along the border of the Basin and the banks of the Grand Canal, it was some five kilometres long, something exceptional for Europe at this time. Alongside the original canals, fruits of the Laguna's natural geometry, the Venetians added others, by way of rationalizing communications for the nerve-centres of the commerce coming from the mainland, the sea, the other lagoon-side trading posts.

That singular Venetian morphology, in which everything is adapted to the placid and steady rhythm of human footfall and the thrust of the oar, was now at the peak of its development. In the city where distances seemed greater than they actually were, the complicated network of *calli* and canals always provided a short and efficacious route between the furthest points. Perhaps uniquely in the world, Venice could not be identified as a centre surrounded by periphery: all of the urban construction was an undifferentiated whole where every rank and role mixed more and more intimately with every other. There was a caste of nobles dedicated, and very knowledgeably, to commerce; and a mass of indigenous people mingled with others of the most diverse provenance, all able to slave and suffer anything in the name of earnings.

At the beginning of the thirteenth century, Europe, newly emerging from the Middle Ages, saw the East as something to be conquered, and from this perception came the later, more mercenary Crusades. In the fourth of them, in 1204, Venice was a protagonist, ready to gamble her whole destiny on a single card. An army of 35,000 men, thousands of horses, and victuals enough to feed such a force for a year were assembled; 300 and more were the ships rigged out by *La Serenissima* for the conquest of the Holy Sepulchre. The crusaders crossed a sea black with ships toward Byzantium, instead; Byzantium would never recover from this. As the Eastern Roman Empire sank, its old vassal city on the lagoon prepared to become *La Dominante*, the dominator of this whole vast Mediterra-

*"... the vast tower of St. Mark seems to lift itself visibly forth from the level field of chequered stones; and, on each side, the countless arches prolong themselves into ranged symmetry, as if the rugged and irregular houses that pressed together above us in the dark alley had been struck back into sudden obedience and lovely order ..." (John Ruskin, The Stones of Venice, v.2)*

*In the tenth century the six boroughs that would make up Venice already existed: Olivolo and Gemini, in the eastern part; Rivoalto, at the centre, including San Marco; Luprio, at the point where the Grand Canal, crossed on horseback, would be widest; Canaleclo toward the northwest; and Dorsoduro, in the strip that overlooks La Giudecca.*

nean basin, the centre of the world.

The city's new growth was more and more in stone. The old pile-embankments that had begun by holding the primitive huts up over the water, became long pales, trunks of an immense and unimaginable forest that, planted deeply in the mud, provided a foundation for ever-more sumptuous palaces. The great arches and long rows of porticos that embellished them represent not only the triumph of void over plenitude, an exalted influence of airy Eastern architecture; they are also a showcase for displaying, along the principal avenue of the Canal, the infinite variety of merchandise on offer in the great Venetian emporium.

Shortly before the sixteenth century the construction of bridges, up to now low and level to facilitate passage to horses, began to be more bowed so that the gondolas could pass below without the boatman's needing to bow. Once more, the form of Venice bent to the exigencies of a world made of water.

In 1492 Christopher Columbus initiated the discovery of the New World. In 1501 Venetians learned that seven Portuguese caravels had succeeded in rounding the southernmost point of Africa, and in making a landing in the Indies. A few years later the Spaniard Cortez would return to Europe with a boatload of easy, if bloody, treasures. From here on the Mediterranean would no longer be the centre of the world and Venice would begin to be a troubled and unsteady queen.

Jacopo da' Barbari, creator of the magnificent bird's-eye map called *Venetie MD*, gives an incredibly sincere and detailed portrayal of the city of these times. It is the encomium of a complete urban creation, with its noble features ardently projected on a future destiny.

The destiny, however, was not to be relied upon. The story as it turned out was that of a slow, luxurious, ineluctable decline, which would modify profoundly the appearance of the Venetian islands.

Sixteenth-century Venice was by now well burdened with history, and honoured and flattered by the contemporary world's greatest men. But it was dizzily losing the power that made it *La Dominante*. The form of the city became more sumptuous, on a scale that confirmed the inordinate civility in which she takes such pride, the civility of the "good life", but it was also aimed as part of her arduous struggle to maintain a credible dignity in a political-economic competition in which she was now nothing

more than a minor player. In the hands of the great architects of the time she became the site of bold experiments in Renaissance, then Baroque building. Venice now scarcely belonged to the merchants and bold sailors, but rather to the great families of the nobility, whose goal seemed to be to squander, in the superficiality of luxury and ostentation, the accumulated riches of the past.

The city beautified herself for herself or for whoever wanted to look at her. She offered herself, ever more generously, to anyone disposed to forget the dignity of the past, content to admire her charms merely, though they may be of an aging beauty prey to illusions, with a pathetically short memory.

It was one long party, and it lasted, constantly more grotesquely, until the twilight of the Enlightenment. The eighteenth century, in the end, gave Venice one last Doge, a dastardly and incompetent Doge, who put an end to her history by surrendering her, without the striking of a single blow, into the hands of Napoleon and the Austrians.

This theatre on the water was much renovated, under the rational if sometimes radical guidance of the philosophers. Nothing but monuments remain of the buildings of the eleventh century, and much has been demolished to make room for new monuments to the new agents of history. A summary example might be the Palazzo Reale, made to twist the great Piazza San Marco and the ancient power into a new perspective. Near the city's edges, the destruction of many ecclesiastical buildings and of whole working-class neighbourhoods made space for the parks near the end of Castello, and the royal gardens, while the broad avenues carved the old civic tissue into rectangles, laying out incongruously straight paths to improve the access from periphery to centre.

Inevitably, as the role of the city changed so did its form. Now what counted was to bring the human and mercantile flux more efficiently to the centre: the city was furnished with vast port entries, fortified islands and barracks; wide streets cut into the live body, with the vacuous additions of sumptuous parks destined, first of all, for neglect and then for vulgar development that was totally estranged from the historical context.

And then, alas, was born the dreadful phantasm of the museum-city, when the nature of Venice as island was forever ended: the Austrians, so wonderfully efficient, so hardworking, so farsighted, killed it by giving *La Serenissima* a railway bridge linking her to the mainland. This line ends on the Grand Canal, next to the wound of the Strada Nuova. Progress now proclaimed itself right into the city, a composite of noise, crowding and hurry, of diligent indifference to the true rhythms of Venice, those of the centuries of lost grandeur. But on the other hand, the centuries themselves being lost, what was there to do? For centuries the Grand Canal had a single bridge; now it had two more, one communicating with the railway station and one built of wood, because it was only a provisional structure; but it has been there so long that there are now people who consider it beautiful. And over the minor canals there appeared iron bridges that seem almost gracious today with the lacy designs of their friezes—and they certainly speed up the traffic.

This is very nearly the form of Venice in our own century, as the previous one had planned it when they endowed the city with perspectives in harmony with the present: a great harbour, a railway station for channelling the movement of products inland, a historic centre prepared to absorb, easily, the industrial-scale aggression of the tourist masses, built-up or buildable zones for the malls and plazas of a city as the moderns understand it.

Other than that, in the present, there is only a greater decadence, bearing witness to illusions lost, because they were false, or merely because they were poorly followed up. Let us put our faces to the window one more time, from the heights. From above one sees none of the aggression of the crowds on the pavement, no more than an intuition in the agitated coming and going of water-craft that shake the banks and the ancient decaying groundwork with their wakes. Nor can we see that in the brief span of 40 years the resident population has thinned to a few tens of thousands of survivors; well-fed, at any rate, since very many of them live off the abundance of tourism. But the form of the city, today, is sad. Sad not with a Romantic abandon, but with death. And yet in the beautifully arranged disarray, and indeed in the desire for life that glances from the azure surfaces of the swimming pools that have covered the ancestral gardens, there is something that is alive.

From on high, one sees. It is the shape of a perhaps pathetic hope, perhaps re-emergent, perhaps on its way to being annihilated. It is the shape of a history of beauty and charm, stone-permanent in a city miraculously suspended in a balance between light and water; a dark shadow of shapes washed by a golden sea. A uselessly majestic sunset, or a dawn, even one that carries nothing but hope?

On the side of Venice facing
the Basin of San Marco, Riva
degli Schiavoni represents one
of the most enchanting walks
in the city. It seems that in the
most ancient times there was
no bank, and the houses stood
directly over the water; later
on, the area was defended
against pirates by a wall.

*The most famous view of La Serenissima: the Palace of the Doges, the domes of the tutelary saint's church, the prisons, the Mint, the Campanile, the Moors' Tower and the two columns of San Todaro and the ferocious lion; before, the kiss of the Basin against the embankments; behind, the houses of workers and artisans.*

The San Marco we see today was consecrated in 1094, in the time of Doge
Vitale Falier. The romanesque skeleton of the basilica approaches a Greek
style, and the five domes—three central and two lateral—were perhaps
proposed on an Eastern model to the unknown architect.

*This church [San Marco], like every great poetic work, is a mystery that defeats narration. What is known of her formation and the thousand things that can be read in her form are insufficient to define her in her essence of life and beauty. … Gothic in the full sense, the aedicules, spires, statues and rampant scrolled foliage were later set up, in the first half of the fifteenth century, to adorn the upper part of the facade." (Diego Valeri)*

For almost exactly 500 years the two Moors have been signalling the passage of time by beating on the great tower bell that takes its name from them. A little below the winged lion holds the gospel open between its paws under a heaven of gilded stars: "Pax tibi, Marce, evangelista meus [Peace to thee, Mark, my Evangelist]."

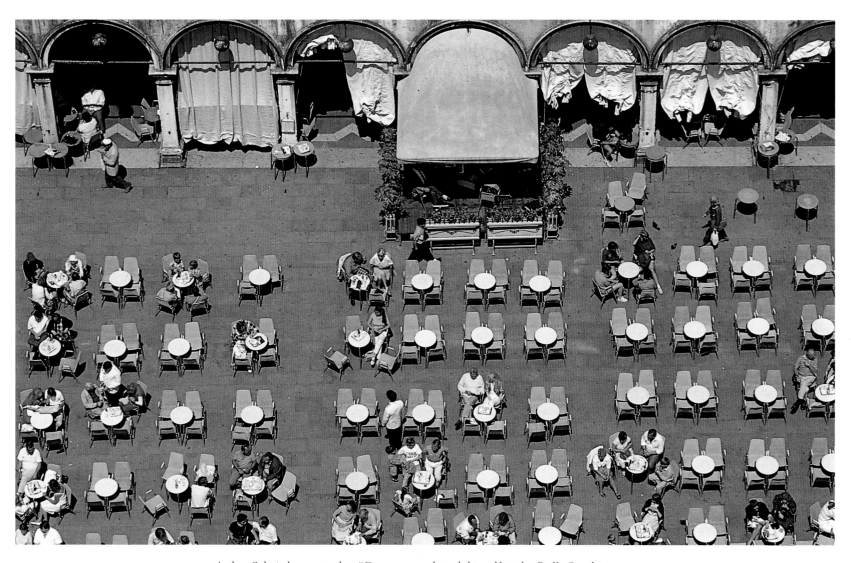

*Arthur Schnitzler wrote that "Casanova ... betook himself to the Caffé Quadri in Piazza San Marco, held to be the principal meeting place of freethinkers and subversives." He returned to Venice as a spy, to persuade himself that "intrigue is the only enticing form of life." Is this what these porticos and festive tables know?*

Looking at the picture, it is hard to imagine a time when Piazza San Marco was an enormous grassy clearing, with trees even, entered on horseback. The narrower side was closed when Napoleon built the Palazzo Reale here, as a sign of the new power at the heart of La Serenissima.

*Riva degli Schiavoni (the bank of the Slavonians) is a passage that leads toward the zone of Castello, facing to the Basin. Very long ago the houses stood directly over the water: then the mall was built, named after the Dalmatians who came from Slavonia to moor their ships here.*

*Open air and the wake of the lighter-craft—to the Punta della Dogana! Place of words inflamed in the daytime by the sun of the whole Basin of San Marco; in the evening, place of whispered words, caresses given or stolen, place of love for the young couples secluded in the sympathetic bosom of darkness.*

."… And when at last the boat darted forth upon the breadth of the  silver sea, across which the front of the Ducal Palace, flushed with its sanguine veins, looks to the snowy dome of Our Lady of Salvation [Santa Maria della Salute], it was no marvel that the mind should be so deeply entranced by the visionary charm of a scene so beautiiful and so strange …" (John Ruskin, The Stones of Venice, v.2)

The Grand Canal is the most important waterway of the city and divides it into two parts of three sestieri each. This is the first section, from the Basin of San Marco until near the bridge. There are three bridges across the Grand Canal: but the Rialto was the only one until the nineteenth century. The other two are recent; Ponte dell'Accademia, in wood (1932) and Ponte degli Scalzi, the "Bridge of the Barefoot", in stone (1934).

*The sinuous banks of the Grand Canal bear witness to its origins as the meanderings*
*of a natural river. At first it was called Canalis Canalecli, and then the sumptuosity*
*of the waterway flanked with the most splendid of palaces made it Grand, or,*
*as the Venetians put it in their own affectionate patois, Canalazzo.*

Along the section of the Grand Canal from the Rialto Bridge almost to the church of
Santa Maria della Salute, one of the monuments is the facade of the Gallerie dell'Accademia (top centre). From here the Bridge of the Accademia crosses the canal
to the open spaces of Campo di Santo Stefano.

On the right rises the potent mass of Palazzo Grassi, now the site of important exhibits under the promotion of the Agnelli Foundation. Left, just at the mouth of the canal that leads toward Piazzale Roma, is the succession of three buildings where the University of Venice has its principal seat: Ca' Foscari.

*Two great palazzi with their white facades, just at the centre: Ca' Pesaro (right),*
*home of the Museum of Modern Art and Ca' Corner della Regina (left) where,*
*in recent years, rich audiovisual documentation has been gathered for*
*the Historical Archive of Contemporary Arts.*

*Rialto? Despite the Tribunal's bulk on the arches of its long portico, it is not a majestic place. It is the lively market of greengrocers and fishmongers, who line up their wares under the tents spread in the open. Their boats, crowded together, overflow with fresh life and colour.*

Piazzale Roma ends the road link to the mainland. If along her canals Venice is populated with coloured boats, this place is populated with thousands of colourful and noisy objects which we call automobiles—part of a present that hurtles ever more violently against the city of silence.

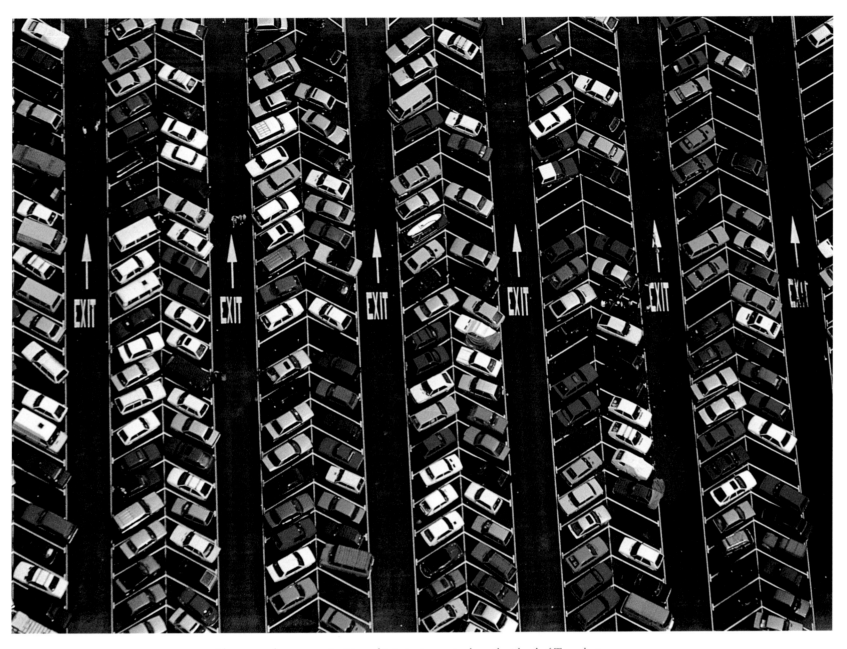

*Almost an abstract composition, this imposing carpark on the island of Tronchetto was constructed entirely to serve the needs of visitors to the city. It is situated next to the commercial port.*

The vast piazzale of the railway station and the Bridge of the Scalzi speak of a modern Venice, of the time in the last century when Austrian dominance called for the city to be linked to the mainland by a bridge. It ended, eternally, the nature of the island as island—the present began.

*Before the present stone arch, this place had a straight iron bridge from a design by
E.H. Neville. It was required by the Austrian administration to provide a more
efficient link between the city centre and the railway station;
the station piazzale can be seen at right.*

*In Carpaccio's "Miracle of the Cross", painted toward the end of the fifteenth century, the Rialto Bridge can be seen still made of wood. Next-door were still to come the Palazzo dei Camerlenghi and the German warehouses of Titian and Giorgione. The wooden bridge collapsed in 1524, the present-day one dates to 1588.*

"… the shadowy Rialto threw its colossal curve slowly forth from the palace of the Camerlenghi, that strange curve, so delicate, so adamantine, strong as a mountain cavern, graceful as a bow just bent … " (John Ruskin, The Stones of Venice)

This little island that supplied Venice's first name (Rivoalto) was the heart of the vast empire of La Serenissima: the routes of the ships that set out from here were like the veins in which the vital fluid of commerce ran that brought riches, splendour and the East to the city of the Doges.

**Above:** *The Riva degli Schiavoni is where the galleys of distant centuries used to drop anchor. Today there are tugboats for ocean-going ships and the various public service craft that keep Venice in communication with the Lido.*
**Below:** *The commercial port is lined with buildings along the canal of the Giudecca, but the great bulk of the ships almost hide the buildings of the city. It is from here that ferries loaded with goods and passengers leave for Greece, Turkey, Yugoslavia and Spain.*

*Just beyond the piazzale of the railway station is the tidy triangle created by the Grand Canal on the right side, Lista di Spagna (once the Spanish embassy) on the left, and at the base, the beginning of the Cana- regio river. Here is the marvellously lovely seventeenth-century Palazzo Labia, now the headquarters of local radio and television broadcasting.*

An anonymous part of the city gathered on the side nearest the mainland. The wooden bridge connects Sacca San Girolamo, an island recently arisen on rubbish (right), with the Baia del Re. Once it was a place of many shipyards, and there are still some among the mass of working-class houses.

La Salute, the Seminary, the first section of the magazines of the Dogana da Mar: in the triangular neighbourhood of these buildings—in connection with the construction of the spendid basilica—to consolidate the terrain they planted a good million and four hundred thousand piles in the mud, an immense forest.

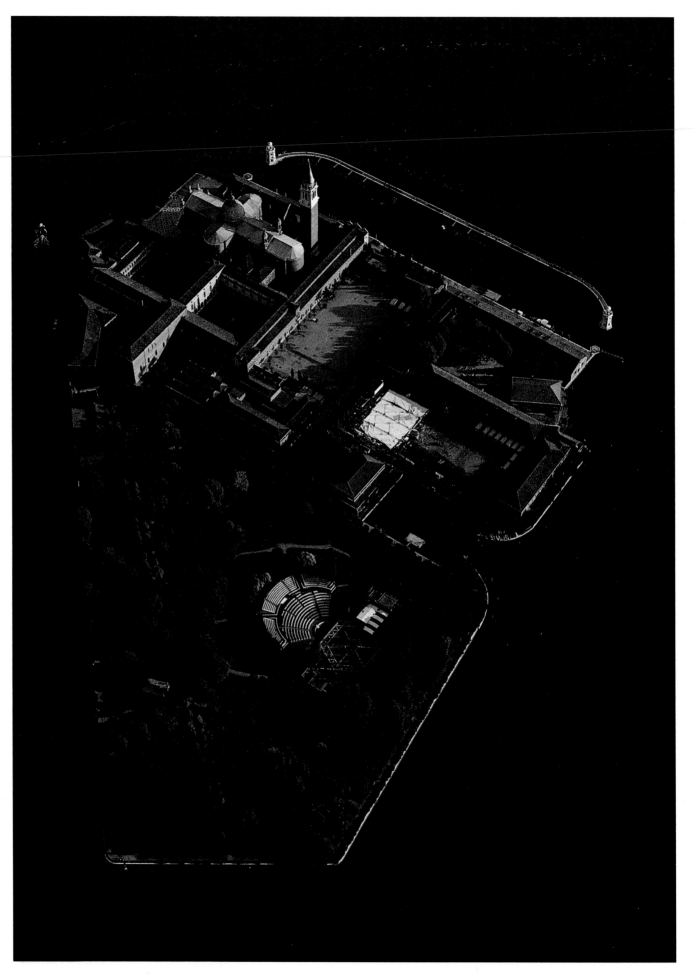

About a kilometre and a half from Olivolo (today San Pietro di Castello) a monastery was set up on the island of San Giorgio Maggiore. Almost at the same distance from Olivolo was another monastery at San Servolo and still another in San Zaccaria.

*The fact that the borough of Olivolo has a port suggests an entire system of support bases for maritime communications between the Levant and the mainland. This was the place that played Venice's international role when Venice herself was just beginning to exist.*

The island of San Pietro di Castello stands out distinctly from the body of Venice. It was called Castrum Helibolis or the Isle of Olivolo, and in the second half of the eighth century it became the seat of the Venetian duchy.

"The patriarchical church, small and architecturally mediocre, stands on the last little island of the Venetian group, and its name, like that of the place where it stands [San Pietro di Castello], is probably unknown to most of the travellers who visit Venice." (John Ruskin, The Stones of Venice, v. 2)

One comes out here on the Fondamenta Nuove to put Venice behind
oneself and take in the perspective of the whole northern lagoon. This
fragment of city never existed until the end of the sixteenth century.
The boat that has just detached itself from the bank is making for
Murano, Burano and Torcello.

The lining up of boats on the bank, here broken and there in a perfect file— these too, each with its own necessary and secret logic, share with Venice a form dictated by the sea.

The form of Venice seems to stagnate, immutable, for ever. And yet it is never the same. Thus here is the satisfaction of discovering, of intuiting between the spaces and the shadow, the ghost that haunts an exterior beauty from within which the intimate will of a creator spiritus glimmers.

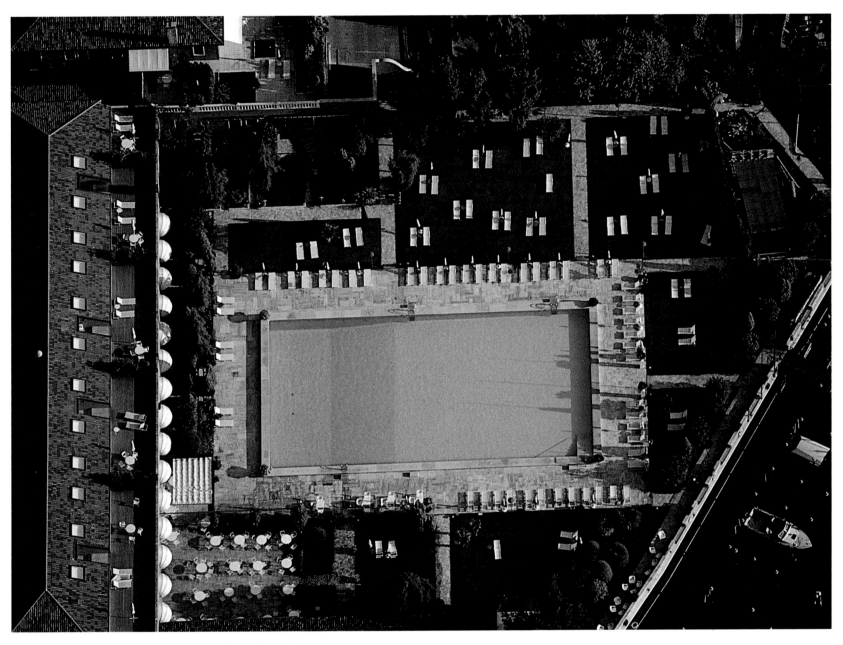

*The great blue mirror dominating the picture is the swimming pool of Hotel Cipriani,
situated at the end of the island of the Giudecca just across from that of San Giorgio
Maggiore: a very peaceful corner for the guest who is acquainted with luxury.*
**Overleaf:** *A sea of gold washes over the phantasm set on a forest of piles buried in
mud: weak, plundered and silent, but caught in a moment of sovereign beauty.
Uncertain, we wonder which is the shadow and which is the light.*

# ISLANDS OF LIGHT

Not far from Venice is a grounded ship hiding a treasure. If we go to Venice to ask her to reveal her secrets of evanescent images, visions, apparitions of a past that still pervades the city on the water and constitutes its real fascination, then we must first come to know Torcello, which is the queen of the Laguna.

A small island, nowadays, with rare houses and few inhabitants, but once, in the earliest times, it was imposing and fairly picturesque, created by the men who abandoned the Roman cities on the mainland in flight from the waves of barbarians, keeping the beauty of the ravaged villas in their minds' eye. Anyone who escapes today from the crowds of tourists in Venice and takes the boat trip from the Fondamente Nuove to the islands of the northern lagoon enters, having left Murano and Burano behind, upon a space made only of water and a rise here and there of mud and shrubbery, a purely horizontal landscape.

But let it be known that within this nothingness there once stood houses, palazzi, churches, with roads and public squares where the people swarmed. None of it is left now, or rather what is left is this great grounded ship that rises like a unique contradiction of the horizon. It is the church of Santa Maria Assunta. It is like a ship with a cargo of time, placed here for eternity. Its treasure is composed of an enormous quantity of little square-cut stones, the tiles of gold, stone and glass of an immensely beautiful mosaic. Entering, you are overwhelmed by the magnitude of these walls, of which every square inch is enriched with mosaic; it is exhausting to try to understand. It is not one single image, but is made of an extraordinarily varied series of stories expressed through forms, figures, colours, embellished with complicated and fascinating symbols. What it narrates is basically as simple as possible: the story of the Universal Judgment. As simple as possible, no doubt, because it is abstract and far away from us, and yet it is so rooted in our deepest ego that it leaves us stupefied, once we are moved to think about it.

Perhaps it would be better to go away, on tiptoe, without understanding. Or perhaps it would be a good moment to have a look and then file away the superficial image among our other memories. Otherwise Torcello will act on us like a poison, slow, subtle and potent, to the effect that Torcello will never leave us; we can flee from here, but here we will return to understand more, to revisit these scenes of the Universal Judgment that we will never fully comprehend, but which have nevertheless become a part of us, a disturbing part.

Shall we visit her, this ship? We will find, certainly, the apotheosis of a great symbol of divinity. But, above all, we will encounter the great matter of myths, the desires, illusions, vices and virtues of humankind. Because this mosaic is first, and for ever, until the sea shall bury the ship, the exaltation of humanity's earthly existence, its way of being in the arduous world, always on the alert, poised between the serene and the utterly lost, the expansively cruel and expansively generous; longing for truth and addicted to the stupidest temptations; always ready to run away from suffering, to create a suffering of one's own, and to be amazed by the mystery of it all. The roads to the heart's desire are always long ones. Now we know that one of them passes through Torcello.

Light, the only light that is always truthful, inhabits Burano. The island is one big painting, a picture animated with concrete life, which walks about here in the guise of so many little protagonists of a play continually being re-written by a happy artist. Looking from above, we can see how it is possible for a city to emerge from the water; indeed we seem to see it surging beneath our eyes, so evident is its aqueous origin. The houses are still massed on islets of grass and mud, as if stone had suddenly and strangely begun to grow out of them. A few watery veins, the canals, divide them, and there is one broad street and a piazza that must have been water itself not long ago. There is yet space for some trees, and boats take a quiet break near the shores. Round about are other islets where stone has not taken the trouble to emerge.

Then, from a closer view, we realize that it is not made just of light; it is made of colours. The colours cry out here, loud and clear; the place is always somewhat theatrical and we must remember that we are on a kind of stage where everything is bedizened with gestures and sonorities that are natural, doubtlessly, but a little stentorian all the same.

We come nearer yet. The reds, the yellows, all the imaginable azures and deep blues cover the fronts of the houses in the tidiest straight lines, hide themselves behind every little curve, and it's always a surprise. Where did these colours come from? From the artist's eyes of a people that had seen nearly everything there was to see in the universe, even if it was only the tiny, but complete, universe of the Laguna. They had seen joy, mist, loneliness, fear, toil. These are the colours of which Burano is

*Are we flying over the countryside? No, this is the island called Le Vignóle. Very near to Venice, it was a holiday place in past centuries and is today intensively cultivated. The name derives perhaps from the broad and fertile vineyards which produced a white wine that kept the rough flavour of brackish water.*

made. Often, travelling, one notices people with the habit of painting their boats in many colours, here as well: so, why not use the same colours on the houses? They too were of wood, at least originally, and then the tradition continued. And why should it not be so, on the island of the truly truthful light? Nearby, in Torcello, the great mosaic was made of the same colours, and the people of Burano went there to pray: they saw the way the tiny spaces sparkled with variegated light: and they used those colours for their houses, their boats, their sails—they brought the story of a Universal Judgment dealing with everyday life into their own everyday lives.

Murano extends almost to the point of touching Venice, neatly divided into several islands by broad canals that, like the Grand Canal, mirror the forms of noble palaces—now in some disrepair. At the centre, behind the long clumsy hangars of the glassworks, rises the jewel of San Donato, a church as old as that of San Marco in Venice, still very beautiful and rich in treasure. The island found its vocation, or rather a vocation was imposed on it, when in 1295 *La Serenissima* decided to transfer all glass-making activities here, out of fear that continuous large fires could endanger the city.

Thus Murano became one of the world's few capitals of that curious art of encircling the air with a most subtle veil of coloured light: glass. And it was apparently well loved: "There were sumptuous palaces where nobles came for summer holidays, where the erudite enjoyed blissful idleness, where ladies could surround themselves with famous suitors, and gardens that, according to all contemporary witnesses, had no peer among ancients or moderns, earthly paradises thanks to the charm of the air and the site, a place of nymphs and demi-gods. Between the island and the city there was a constant coming and going, during the season, of boats ornamented with people who were themselves rather ornamented, the figures of courtiers, scholars, ladies, and cavalieri that we can see in our minds as Tintoretto and Veronese painted them." (J. Filiasi)

The flight is quick and easy over the island of San Michele, which offers a last shelter to those who have finished their earthly pilgrimage. Originally it was two islands; the other was called San Cristoforo della Pace. They were merged when Napoleon ordered in the Edict of Saint Cloud that cemeteries were to be transferred well beyond the centres of their cities. In the corner nearest to Murano stands the lovely church of San Michele in

*Torcello has the fascination of necessary places, those that impose respect and silence. Then they give you everything, but only in exchange for all of yourself, without reserve. Some have come here to stay forever, even surrounded with modern amenities next to the ancient relics.*

Isola, the first example, and still one of the most notable, of Renaissance religious architecture in the entire lagoon.

Venice has more than one beach; they are what sets a limit to the lagoon, keeping it from joining the sea. But the Lido (the Italian name means just "the beach"), is only one of them, the one that provides a space for the white edifice of the Hotel des Bains and that other, absurdly Moorish construction, the Hotel Excelsior. It has seen better days, when it was frequented by what would now be called the jet set; those were the times of Thomas Mann or, in any case, his character Gustav Eschenbach, who found there an outlet for his mad desires, and wretchedness in consequence. What has changed, from Mann's description given in *Death in Venice?* "The sand was burning hot. Awnings of rust-coloured canvas were spanned before the bathing-huts, under the ether's quivering silver-blue; one spent the morning hours within the small square shadow they purveyed. But the evening too was rarely lovely: balsamic with the breath of flowers and shrubs from the nearby park, while overhead the constellations circled in their spheres, and the murmuring of the night-girt sea swelled softly up and whispered to the soul. Such nights as these contained the joyful promise of a sunlit morrow, brimful of sweetly ordered idleness, studded thick with countless precious possibilities."

And Diego Valeri adds: "Everything is more than sufficiently ugly; but the sea is there, with its golden sand (the gentlest skin in the world)."

If you follow from beach to beach toward the south, you arrive at Chioggia. This settlement, older than Venice, had the misfortune, as its destiny, to be too closely attached to the mainland, and to serve as the first bulwark against any and all invaders. It looks utterly orderly, in the almost geometric form of the canals and streets that divide it up, but actually it is rather wild, a little chaotic, as though it were perpetually on the point of weighing anchor. Many of the inhabitants dwell in that same state, still living on fishing, and in fact the canals are populated with every form and colour of marine life. Whoever remains on land turns out, at five in the evening, along the principal street, for the rite of the *passeggio*, the classically Italian evening promenade, and for the opportunity to discuss whatever happens in this happily rustic atmosphere.

And hereafter there are no more islands, nor is there any more lagoon.

*A comprehensive view of Torcello and the surrounding territory: the Della Rosa marshes open up above right; below, connected by a narrow road running along a dyke, is the island of San Pieretto, inhabited today by members of the yoga-and-macrobiotic-diet cult.*

Torcello might have been the true centre of the Laguna, if it could have been defended better from the invaders massed on the mainland. It had perhaps 50 churches and 30,000 inhabitants. Now nothing is left but the first church, a little Eastern jewel that is nearly 1,000 years old.

The colours of Burano are in a single island no larger than the Piazza del Duomo in Milan. They dwell among a civil and spontaneous people in a place where beauty is not "art", but always the unequivocal beauty of a port where it is "beautiful" to lay anchor.

*The exaggerated red of a sunset, the delicate azure of dawn, the deepest blue of the
sea, the piercing green of gardens—then you find the same colours stolen from the
lagoon to be placed over people's doorways. Burano has the fascination of a
symphony of variegation.*

Burano has just one piazza, placed at the end of its single broad street, which retains something of a canal in its shape. The street is named Via Baldassare Galuppi, after the musician, an illustrious representative of the sixteenth-century Venetian school, who was born here.

The picture shows Burano in its truest details: the groups of simple but perfectly restored houses, the wide walks of the piazza and streets that were once canals, the boats moored just outside the doors, and the exultation of the colours framing the thousand windows of the fisherfolk.

The legend of Burano's famous lace, the merletti: a sailor from here met the Sirens
on his travels, but he knew how to resist them. Their queen, enchanted, pulled a
garland of foam from the sea, with a sweep of her tail, and gave it to the handsome
youth to give his own sweetheart as a bridal veil.

**Overleaf:** "This island had the name Buriano, one of the ports of the already destroyed Altino, and over it the Buriana family built Burano, which the Latins called Burianus." They say that Buranello was nearby, "an island of small circumference, whose vestiges can be seen under the water, when it is clear." (J. Filiasi)

"*Your homes recall the nests of marine birds, now set on the ground and now floating on the surface of the water, according to the rhythm of the tides ... At every door a boat is tied like an anxious or a patient domestic animal.*" (Cassiodorus, minister of the Emperor Theodoric)
**Following double page:** *A distressingly modern intervention in the amiable texture of Burano and next-door Mazzorbo: perhaps a condominium designed by Snow White, or a little child's-brick model of it.*

*The boat that links Venice to Murano, Burano and Torcello glides impressively over the Mazzorbo Canal. On board, as always, is the most disparate list of goods for sale, as if it were a gypsy caravan. In the most secluded places, the mist from outside and the smoke of the rowdy passengers inside are indistinguishable.*

A minuscule island of very minor history is that of Madonna del Monte. A little nuns' convent, then the dwelling of a few hermits, and in our century a powder magazine which looks completely ruined today. A legend mentions a sound of raucous gasping that sometimes rises from the water.

*Preceding pages:* Murano looks enormous in the foreground; at left appears San Michele and behind it the port of Venice connected by a subtle ribbon of road to the mainland, where the white smokestacks of the industrial zone gleam on the horizon.

*"Murano too has its Grand Canal, which winds between collapsing old palaces and jolly little cottages. A convent wall here and there preserves the memory of an intense spiritual life and at the same time of grandiose, Casanovan turpitude."*
(Diego Valeri)

Like Venice, Chioggia has had its shape determined almost entirely by the will of nature: a few islands rising out from between narrow canals. Here too the houses grew on a foundation of great piles buried in the mud.

*Chioggia is made of long islands neatly separated by straight canals. In the centre is the principal avenue, forever crowded with people. The bobbing fishing boats, always ready to leave, are still the main livelihood of the inhabitants of this last island of the southern lagoon.*

With Murano in the background, very near the edge of Venice; spreads the island of San Michele. It is the island of the Dead, the lagoon's ultimate retirement home. Giorgio Baffo said of this destiny: "E come da 'sto mar tutti nassemo, dopo in 'sto mar tutti tornemo [as we are all born out of this sea, to this sea we all return]."

*The Church of San Michele in Isola was the first religious building to be built between Venice and the lagoon during the Renaissance. By Mario Codussi, it remains one of the most beautiful constructions of the period (1469). The great arch of the cloister, also of the fifteenth century, gives access to the city cemetery.*

Up to today the Hotel Excelsior and the Grand Hotel des Bains present an appearance almost the same as they had when Thomas Mann described them in 1912. An addition of our time is the modest breakwater, ending in a ring, that helps to prevent the waves from eroding the littoral.

*The Grand Hotel des Bains was constructed to offer the maximum comfort to the refined clientele that owners hoped to attract to the Lido in an attempt to promote it as a fantastic sea-bathing resort. It is still a very luxurious hotel, retaining the integrity of its lovely turn-of-the-century architecture.*

"A long row of capanne ran down the beach, with platforms, where people sat as on verandahs, and there was social life, ... visits were paid, amid much chatter, punctilious morning toilets hob-nobbed with comfortable and privileged deshabille. On the hard wet sand close to the sea figures in white bath robes or loose wrappings in garish colours strolled up and down." (Thomas Mann, Death in Venice)

*Motorboats skim over the water like dolphins, barely making it ripple, like a flock rushing toward the joy of a nearby shore. Beside, the brilliantly coloured gondolas advance under vigorous oars: a man on the prow, another at the poop—these two have been, for millennia, the motor of the lagoon.*

# FORMS OF THE LAGUNA

How many lagoons are there, beneath this water and this mud? For thousands of years the lagoon was nothing but a complex of water, earth, light, plants and animals—simply someplace in the world, living inside time and through the seasons. There were people as well, of course, but there was certainly not much they could do to change it. A little at a time, however, they managed: fishermen, peasants, salt miners, refugees, and who knows who else, started a new life by setting up stunted stilt houses. Until, on top of a grandiose forest of piles, Venice herself arose, supremely beautiful and powerful, and not finished even today.

The formation of the lagoon was extremely complex, but we can sum it up by thinking of a series of rivers that, flowing into the sea, scattered the detritus they carried until they created a line of littorals; broken at intervals, defining the boundaries of a vast internal basin. The action of sea, wind, tides and rivers, produced an environment of constantly unstable, delicate balance.

The basin of our own time, contained in the northeast by the river Sile and in the southeast by the Brenta, has a surface of about 550 square kilometres: of these, 26 are land that is always above the surface, that is the islands; 92 are more slippery outcroppings, the *barene* that remain visible when the tides stay within their normal range, and the *velme* that are submerged at every high tide. The other 432 are covered with water. The lagoon is separated from the sea by a row of beaches, divided at three points: the entrances of Chioggia, Malamocco and San Nicoló di Lido.

Within, a vast surface of free water, the Laguna is alive, bordering on so many further water-mirrors where the bottom is deeper, adjacent to those "valleys of fish", basins enclosed within artificial dams in order to control influx and outflux as required for the rearing of fish there.

All this water is crossed by a fantastically intricate system of canals. On a development of about 835 kilometres is an alternation between the broad, deep "trunks" that communicate directly with the sea; from these you can trace the "primary branches" that, branching more and more deeply into the basin, gradually change, giving birth to a kind of capillary network, the *ghebbi*, which penetrate to the most hidden spots.

It is a shame to say nothing but this sort of thing, indispensable as such information may be in coming to an understanding of the Laguna's ambience. One is always touched with a desire to dwell more at length on the lagoon, *con amore*, on its flitting changes of form and colour, its stubborn permanences, its vexing instability, because it is the interpenetration of all these elements that lends life to forms and proportions of pure beauty and harmony. If some respectful advice may be offered, looking at the images that lie before us in these pages: let us not devote all our attention to the principal subject, but rather observe, at length, the background details. We will thus realize how none of these forms is ever fortuitous, but that all possess the subtle vitality of the handiwork of nature. Let us look exactly where it seems unimportant to look; we will see the little secrets beneath the appearances emerging, a little at a time, and we will understand that this is the delicate and shifting living intrigue of which the lagoon is made. Perhaps we may also understand a bit more of ourselves, because this lagoon is a demanding world, and a trip down there might well never end at all.

Next to the more famous islands, the crown of Venice, sites still animated by human life or illustrious for their grandiose monuments, is the whole estuary of modest islets where life languishes, or has disappeared, or hardly moves one way or the other. Among these, just opposite Burano, San Francesco del Deserto sends its rows of splendid cypresses heavenward like a prayer: "O blessed solitude, o solitary blessing," reads the motto at the convent entrance. A few gentle and hardworking monks have lived here since 1220, when Saint Francis built himself a little retreat to rest after the fatigues of a preaching tour that had taken him to Egypt and Palestine and borne very little fruit. Becoming uninhabitable on account of environmental conditions, the island was abandoned by the Frati Minori around 1400, then wasted away for centuries until the Austrians turned it into a munitions depot; finally, the brothers returned in 1858, and the complex of monastic buildings was rebuilt in the present form, where peace truly reigns. And it is lovely today to see it surrounded by the truest elements of the lagoon, with this vast perfect meadow that seems to dissolve, almost, in the infinitely varied greens of the water.

Almost opposite the borough of Malamocco, which was a rather important city until Pepin destroyed it in 810, the islet of Povaglia is practically dead. All those buildings, well maintained though they may look, do not count; they are empty and useless. At one time it was used

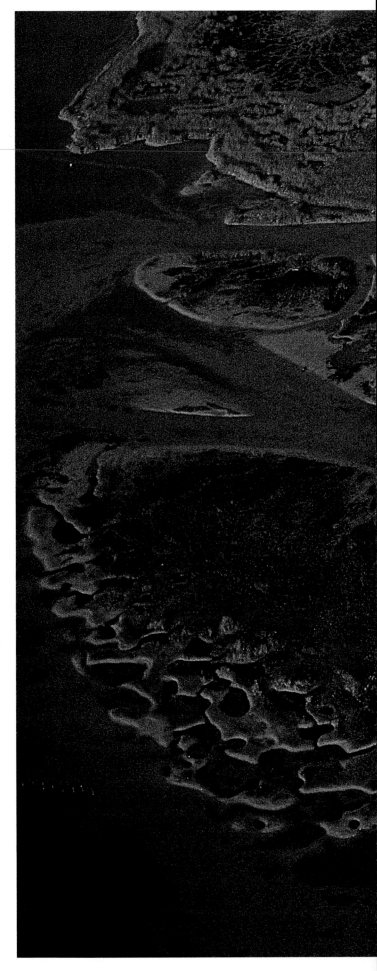

as a *lazaretto* for travellers suspected of contagion, then it became a home for the elderly. Now nothing is left but the outline of the cultivated fields, bearing witness that the island has a right to live better than this. That octagonal island is typical, one of many formed this way at a time when many of the minor islands were used as powder magazines, after it was decided to remove those dangerous depots from Venice.

The isle of San Lazzaro degli Armeni is rich in history and art. The use of part of the island by monks goes back all the way to the fifteenth century; before that, for a long period, it was used as a sanctuary for lepers. After having been the seat of the Dominican fathers, in 1716 it became the refuge of a group of Armenian priests. Venice was always tolerant of all religious professions, as long as there was something to be gained in exchange. When Napoleon entered the city—San Lazzaro being directly across from the Basin of San Marco—the crafty Armenians raised an enormous Muslim banner: the French commander was allied with the Sultan, and while his anticlerical zeal attacked all the rest of the city, he respected these priests. Those of the buildings that are clearly distinguishable, surrounded by meadows and gardens, also house a library of about 30,000 volumes, as well as a virtually unique printing-works that produces books in the characters of almost all the Eastern languages.

At the time when Venice sent pilgrims to the Holy Land on her own galleys, getting, of course, a tremendous profit out of them—and in some respects it was a kind of tourist trip *ante litteram*—San Clemente functioned as a hospital for luckless pilgrims who got sick *en voyage*. Afterwards, it became the place where illustrious guests of Venice were put up, and it may have been none other than an ambassador of the Duchy of Mantua who came in 1630 accompanied by the contagion of a terrible pestilence; when the epidemic was over, it was here that the grateful Venetians erected the Chiesa della Salute.

San Servolo also faces the Basin of San Marco. For 500 years it was the home of Benedictine monks; subsequently, it provided refuge for the nuns escaping from the destruction of Malamocco, then yet another group of nuns who had been chased out of Crete at the hand of the infidel Turks. When there were only four of them left, the sisters were received elsewhere and the island became, as it was until very recently, a hospital. The almost constant utilization of these last islands has kept them

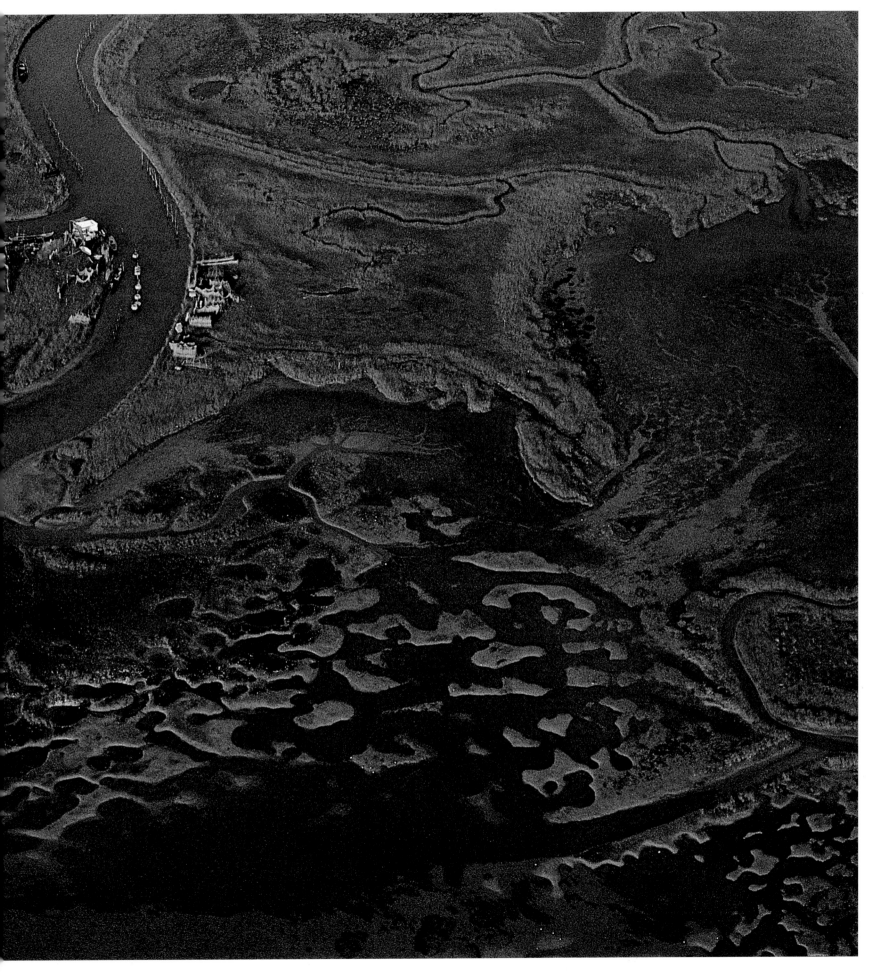

*Can a landscape like this be shaken by storms? And yet Brother Francis of Assisi, coming back on a Venetian ship from a preaching tour of the Levant, found refuge here as a great tempest raged. He built a wretched shelter with his own hands, then took up the performance of miracles.*

from falling in ruin; you can see quite clearly the outlines of the walls that prevent the water from eroding their shores, and from the shallows all round one can see the mud dappled with little zones of subaqueous vegetation.

There were also islands too small to contribute to the needs of religious orders, many of them too far away as well from the historic centre. Such places might still serve for a few farming families; this is the case for little Tesséra. Its almost perfectly semicircular form may be the result of previous wear, as you can see it outlined by a bank of stones that must be the remains of some now-crumbled embankment. But it has its own lively dignity, with its blots of trees, its outbuildings, and the shape of a garden pond near the shore; of more recent construction are the two parallelepipeds of somewhat dubious taste.

Of the islets without any history the most beautiful is perhaps Crevan. Tiny, luxuriantly overgrown, well consolidated with dykes, even if the *barena*-tide behind them looks ready to wash it away, it arouses desire; a very comfortable place to be. Behind, the *barena* is an elegant arabesque, tinted playfully in a thousand different shades. The tide is on the low side just now, the time when the seagulls make their most scrumptious meals, pecking after little fish and molluscs in the mud. If we could look a great deal more closely, we would probably see the white waders that have been returning to populate the lagoon here in the neighbourhood of Burano.

The "valleys of fish" provide a relatively profitable activity in the lagoon. Valle Zappa, in the south zone of the Basin, displays all the clever geometry that has been developed for this delicate work: one can see the weirs that connect it to the outside, the pools created by recent embankment works, still bare of greenery, the floating crane for dragging the bottom and gathering the mud, the various kinds of building from simple sheds to a farmstead to a villa of noteworthy proportions. The light has been obliging today, and it shows us a lagoon of azure water after all the greens and greys of the previous images.

Then, after one of those rare nights when the northeast wind has raged, the Laguna hides itself in fine mist on which the distant snow-capped mountains seem to sit enthroned. It is like an optical illusion, at certain moments; as if they were standing on a lake. But if we add a touch of the light of sunset, and a new veil of mist approaching, we conclude our little trip in an atmosphere out of a dream or fairy tale.

*Brother Francis stuck a stick in the ground—it was cut from Albanian pine. A tree miraculously grew from it, which the Franciscan monks of the island of San Francesco del Deserto have venerated ever since, in memory of the founding saint.*

*San Francisco del Deserto is set in the neighbourhood of Burano and is peaceful to the point of being hypnotic. Next to the slim sharp-pointed belltower is a little church with a fourteenth-century cloister, still intact, where the small community of brothers lives.*

*San Lazzaro degli Armeni, dedicated to the patron saint of lepers, was the landing point in 1716 of an Armenian nobleman Manug di Pietro, nicknamed Mechitar ("the Consoler"), in flight from an invasion of the Turks at Methoni. The island was also one of Lord Byron's favourite places.*

The cultured and enterprising Armenian fathers, finding a refuge in this island of San Lazzaro, now called "degli Armeni" after them, became rich, respected and admired for their printing-works and scholarship. Not by chance, there is a building on the island where one can still be impressed by a ceiling fresco by Tiepolo.

*These two islands are not very congenial to Venetians. There were psychiatric hospitals here for a long time, and that is the source of the joke of questioning the sanity of those mentioning the name of San Servolo or San Clemente.*

*A little after the year 1000 a shelter for pilgrims on the way to the Holy Land was set up on San Clemente. For centuries afterwards it was used by various monastic orders, or hermits. The buildings to be seen now were all built after 1834, for the psychiatric hospital.*

The Doge Pietro Tradonico was killed in one of La Serenissima's not infrequent
rebellions. Almost 200 families of rebels were confined on the island of Poveglia. To
keep them quiet the city granted them considerable privileges, but not enough, and in
1378 had to disperse them still further away.

**Overleaf:** *Next to the islet of Tesséra, on the edge of a broad navigable canal, two water-taxis speed like arrows between Venice and the international airport on the margin of the mainland, in a place with the same name as the islet.*

*This island is called Carbonera and it has a surface area of less than 500 square metres. Its origins are relatively recent; it lies between Murano and the edge of the mainland where the Marco Polo Airport is, and it holds a villa surrounded by the green of woods and orchards.*

*Lazaretto Vecchio, "the old Leprosarium" just opposite the Lido, began historically as
another way-station for pilgrims to Palestine. Later it was a quarantine for people
and merchandise (whence the name), then made over to military uses;
today it is a hospice for stray dogs.*

The marsh zone might seem like a primordial world on a microscope slide, a world at the beginning of life. Then, the luxuriantly grown island shows that plants have appeared on this world already, and man as well, his houses and his boats.

"Valliculture" is the breeding of fish in the "valleys", where one hectare of valley yields up to 150–200 quintals of fish: eel, mullet, bream and bass. In our time, approximately 9,000 hectares have been turned over to this activity, which could mean not only the continuation of an ancient tradition but also a rich future.

*Preceding pages: This veil of friendly and menacing water over which the mist and mountain peaks hang: will it ever again carry history? Perhaps the next chapter will simply be a great submersal, mud will cover the ruins, and silence will reduce the present to memory.*

*Above: The shapes of these small boats are centuries old, though from time to time they have been modified as the technology of fishing changed. They represent the livelihood of many of the inhabitants of the lagoon.*

*Page 144: Like a piece of Venetian lace stretched over the calm water of the Laguna, a system of nets held up by poles stuck in the sea bottom lures schools of fish to pass between the cone-shaped seragie. This too is a witness to the abundance of fish here in the lagoon.*

# INDEX

# ACKNOWLEDGEMENTS

The publisher and Guido Rossi, the photographer, would like to thank the Italian Air Force SMA 2 Reparto for their help. All the photographs were taken with their Concessione SMA No. 694 of 15 July 1987. They are also indebted to Giancarlo Costa for the old maps reproduced on pages 21, 23 and 24–5.
Finally, a special thank-you must be said to His Excellency, Mr. Alessandro Vattani, the Italian Ambassador to Singapore, and his wife, Francesca, for their invaluable assistance.

**Sources of the quotations:**
Thomas Mann: *Thomas Mann's Stories and Episodes*, trans. H.T. Lowe-Porter (Martin Secker and Warburg, 1911)
John Ruskin: *The Stones of Venice*, vol. 1 and 2, Everyman's Library series (J.M. Dent and Sons Ltd., 1907)
**Italian sources:**
Giorgio Baffo: *Poesie* (Venice, 1789)
Jacopo Filiasi: *Memorie storiche dei Veneti primi e secondi* (Venice, 1786)
Arthur Schnitzler: *Il ritorno di Casanova* (Adelphi, Milan, 1988)
Diego Valeri: *Guida sentimentale di Venezia* (Le tre Venezie. Padua, 1949)

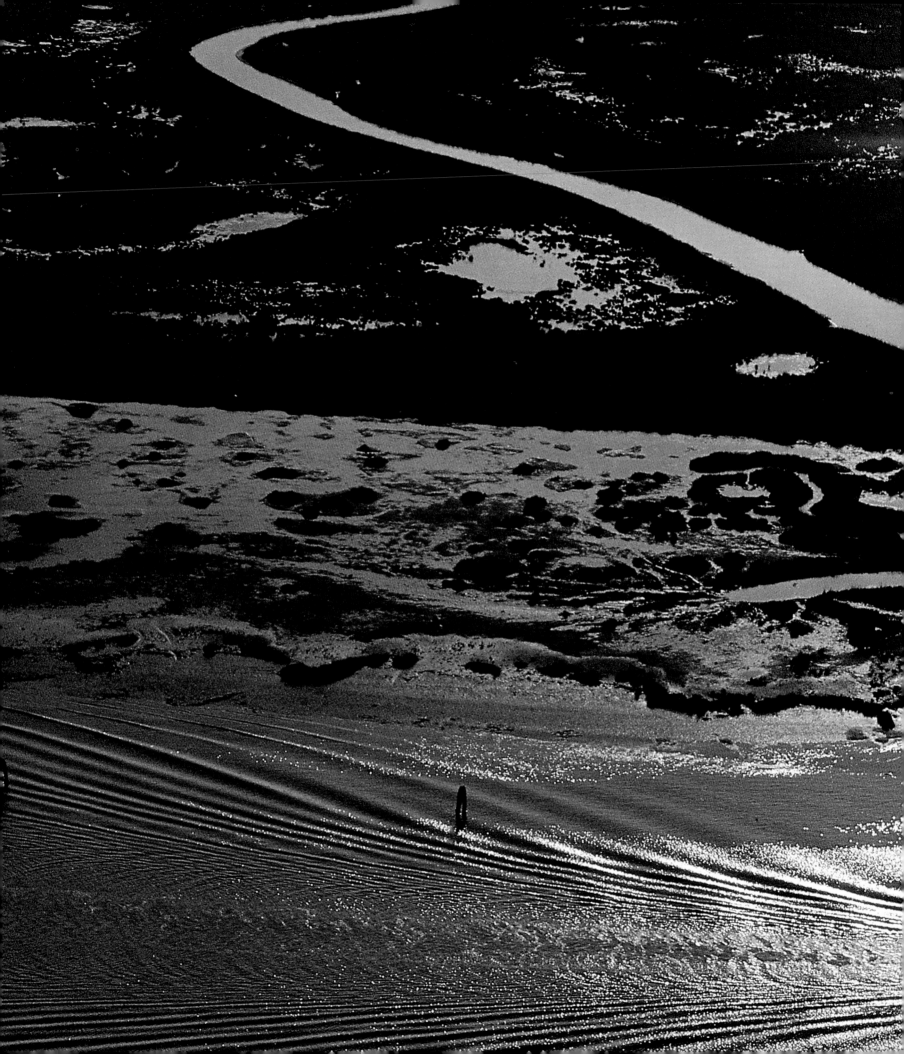